Fallen Petals

Fallen Petals

Poems by

Judith Ann Levison

Cover design by Shay Culligan
Cover art by Judith Ann Levison

ISBN: 978-1-952326-57-8

Kelsay Books
502 South 1040 East, A-119
American Fork, Utah, 84003

For: My husband, Bob
and children, Adam and Ruthie

Acknowledgments

Illuminations: "Beginnings," "Nanny"

Conceit Magazine: "Corn Flakes," "Patio," "Death of a Cowgirl," "The Mermaid"

The Storyteller: "Daddy"

Art Times Magazine: "We Once Were Great Ladies," "Protection," "The Parting," "Red Fox," "Winston Arthur Berry"

Hollins College: "The Caretakers"

Amulet Poetry Magazine: "Old Companion," "Insomnia"

The Awakenings Review: "Fake Leopard Coat," "Horse," "Magical Things," "First Journey"

California Quarterly: "Farewell," "Trucker Dream"

Poem: "Best Friend"

Mudfish: "The Rides"

Haight Ashberry: "The Bed and the Boat"

Poetalk: "Old Bath Road, Maine"

Contents

Beginnings

To my mother I was a blade of grass,
a string bean, someone always
pushing a broom or beating huge
spiders in the rafters.
I was a silent girl. She cursed her opinions openly.
Only in my dreams did she hold my face in her hands,
crooning thanks for my diligence. But alas, I was awoken
to mop at five, before breakfast.

To my father I was invisible,
a quiet girl, braids hanging over
books he only looked at before he died and could not see.
Our food came from hard logging and pouching,
deer hanging in the shed, dripping blood.
Our family money bulged in his drunken brothers' pockets.

In vain my older sister fought back, while my
younger obese sister, in hiding, quietly ate.
I sang folk songs to my infant brother
about love and faraway places.

Corn Flakes

Take one memory and find your place in it.

Never mind the raw ice wind, hold yourself in the malleable center
tight enough to be safe, not thrown into the trees illuminated
by the glassy large moon.

Your father is eating corn flakes at the kitchen table.
Spoon up and down, pipe tobacco scattered around his bowl.

You talk to him of your journeys to and from college on the dirt-
scalded buses. He may not be listening.

Looking far away he is escaping fourth grade out of a broken
window and running through Maine's Dixmont Hills to find his
brothers.

How long should I remain in this picture with its wreath of pines
and the sparkly pitch?

After his death I spoke to him in the ripe green woods
of all my sad imploring glories.

Perhaps he is listening to me mid-sentence.
No, I do not believe that.

Even in death, people never change.

Patio

Why can I not write what I see?
Happiness: my husband and I sitting
on the patio, studying the trees and wildflowers,
naming the bird calls.

Many friends are dying around us. This decade
will be a long road of sorrow as natural
as the screeching blue jay or Black-eyed Susan
curling inward.

Languishing in grief, I blanked pictures from my mind,
repeated prayers to stop the guilt that was its true undercurrent.

In my twenties caring little for life except for college,
I was vulnerable to cruel men, I lived from book
to book. Relationships were momentary and damaging,
until I flew, for the first time, to a new college, a new
life.

On the patio again, we hear a plane overhead from
a nearby airport. Our son is a pilot and we call out
his name: Adam, there is Adam.

Our friends are dying, grandchildren thrive. I came out
of my depression when I saw the Tiger Swallowtail
butterfly taking nectar from the goldenrod.

Long, lonely, peaceful times. We must remember them.

Library Books

An apartment patio window reveals
a thin, tree-lined gorge.
Wild and hungry fall winds sprinkle
yellow leaves to the ground. Shadows
disarm trunks of light. The black
patio set will remain empty; shut-in,
my spirits turn inward.

Every Sunday books are spilled into the
return boxes, more gathered. A McQueen
biography: his "cool" image ending in Mexico,
a stomach tumor removed for death to enter.

Mondrian: flowers, single watercolors,
chilled with opaque ink drawings float off
each page toward surreal meadows.

No returns here as phone relationships lapse
into silence. Next week arms of books must atone.
After all, archival spirits are as genuine as a thousand
mighty autumns, loneliness never past due.

The Sears Catalogue

I always wanted a mother
to part my bangs with her fingers,
braid my hair, not sting it with Toni perms.

But mine was not human, she jumped
when you went near her, snapped foul words
if something moved you on television.
To her love was a filthy rag dissipated
somewhere generations back in a wind
so malicious, your feelings were
ground out like one of her Pall Malls.
She wanted you to die, this is why one
incident will never free me from trembling.
in my "five and dime" innocence.

One quiet Saturday she became unhinged
like a dog grown mad.
She accused me of stealing her red lipstick.

I was reading a Sears catalogue by the wood stove.
She began screaming, moving in a dervish way.
Blinded by the beauty of the dresses and prim coats,
I did not see (or did I?) the stove hook in her hand
come swiftly down upon my head.

I saw the stove far away before I passed out, left the earth,
traveling light years into another brain space,
no more a young girl, but one who saw
the catalog in bits and pieces where I no longer
could be a model with a chiseled red mouth.

Daddy

When you were alive, we never talked.
Hello, goodbye, silent as the trees you felled.
Day after day sawdust flew onto your skin,
you clawed trees aboard a truck, stacking
logs, chaining them.

Your old corn cob pipes
hang in the garage on small pegs.
Dead ten years, I want to ask you questions
of your brutal childhood. Motherless, older brothers
took the cots and left you curled on the floor
winter after winter.

I sent money stipulating it for quilts with a moose
or deer motif. Never warm enough, you
slept days, sat up nights waiting to elude
death before it reached you.

I do not care to mention my passionate wrath
or risks you could not take to save me from
my mother's slapping hand.
To be belittled and cast into disgrace was what you learned.
We never spoke of her hyena's pitch.

I had potatoes and venison, a few clothes, Golden Books,
nail polish. The impoverished cherish and transform
what little they have into emotional treasures.

I had a bride doll with a carrying case.
After she died, you said she was your bride and you loved her.
My love for you real, could it be as twisted?

Old Maid's Tale

When I was twelve, I wanted to be the nun
in "The Nun's Story". The arduous journey,
the conflagrations, and condemnations
appealed to my sinking ego, my guilt for hating home.
I wanted to be anyone but myself: a solitary woman
who like Emily, "never saw the ocean…" although it
was so near, I could hear the waves rising in blue froth,
dragging back a wet hem to leave small shells, a child's
bucket.

My neurotic, addicted family drank and whined.
They needed me for rides, groceries, keeping pills
organized in day-of-the-week plastic squares.

On a whim, I pulled a satin dress over my head,
stuffed it in a pine chest.
Wearing a crown I dreamt of riding a white horse,
as mountains of clouds rushed toward me in mists of lavender---
never landing to again bank fires in the night.

The dream continued for years. Collecting dolls,
postcards, small figurines, an old maid wearing chunky
shoes, a net over a chignon.
Having cried all my life, I never cried after my parents' deaths.

Where are you love, who belongs only to me?
In silent rooms, waves of change rock beneath me.
I wear the satin dress with white slippers in the moonlight.
I loosen my long hair, forgive them and allow
my life to flower.

Overprotected Child

Surprised my mother allowed me to go to the circus,
I boarded the middle school bus one April morning.

My shoes tight, denim jacket a misty blue; an orchid
barrette clipped back unruly bangs. Nervous, I sat behind
Mr. Shea, the bus driver.

Mother was afraid of everything outside, did not drive.
Once I wore a billowy pink blouse, waiting for a ride
at days end. My father came home late from the
lumber yard. After that I did not expect to go anywhere
outside of school.

I followed Mr. Shea, he found seats on the second tier.
The smell of peanuts, popcorn, candy wrappers
mixed with putrid sweat from the crowd sickened me.
The performers looked tired and drab, nothing was colorful.
Noise deafening, I wanted to return home.

The elephants were brought out, feet like large stumps.
I heard the whips sing. After the balancing acts,
one large elephant with a broad tapestry on his back,
a beaded shield on his forehead broke a chain.

The handler beat and beat the agitated elephant,
rearing, lunging toward the man . . . . I shuddered, tried
to yell, but nothing came out, just strange moans.

Mr. Shea asked if I was all right. He sat beside me, gave me
a box of Cracker Jack. They took the elephant away he said.

I understood. With bullies on the playground and mother
at home, you could go berserk.

Cleaning Woman at a Vegas Hotel

I peddle cleanliness
with a cumbersome cart
of bleach and sprays,
linen and towels poke out of every corner
in origami shapes.
Days are longer than my life.
I open and shut the heavy wine curtains
locking smoke, perfume, and bad love
in the rooms.

I know the anguish of the vanished,
the whistle of luck in the bathroom mirror's
casino pool of dreams.
I replace the pillowcase damp with tears,
empty a basket with mascara stained Kleenex.
If I forget a room, Madre's home might again
be walls of newspaper, peeling mold.

My Juan with his precious cigars only lights
false hopes and chronic nostalgia.
Midnight, we say prayers, press close.

We Once Were Great Ladies

It was October, fall's spices in the air.
A disease was attacking the oaks, acorns few,
Squirrels were eating apples.

A large box arrived in the mail from our great aunt.
It was filled with two rose silk dresses, high heels.
Beads of every color, hats that covered our eyes,
Evening gloves, brooches, faceless lockets and the
Most precious item: a large star to pin in your hair.

No room in the house, we dressed up in a murky garage,
Became Louisa May Alcott, the Bronte sisters,
Virginia Wolfe and other esteemed women. We forgot
Our real selves, never allowed to have friends over,
Going for a ride once a week.

Then one breezy day, when colored leaves
Fell in our hair, we saw the box in the pickup truck
To be taken to the dump. A gas scent was in the air.
Father said a can spilled on the clothes.

Conversation always discouraged, we said nothing.

In shock we walked toward the woods and our
Playhouses made of sticks, stones, and several stumps.
We sat in the houses and did not even feel
Like visiting one another.

Something in us died as so often did before.

Protection

My daughter and I sat on her bed
hovering over my fine jewelry,
listening to the jingling sounds, intent
over each piece, pulling the twisted
necklaces apart, shaking the bangles.

Prom night had come and gone.
She bought two dresses, had them taken in,
sequins individually sewn.
But she did not go. There was a misunderstanding.

I never met the boyfriend, could not console
her the night her heart first broke.
I knew she would forget the boy, but not the feeling.

We seldom spoke, perhaps my illness burdened her,
or she was ashamed of my destitute Maine background,
offering no family to embrace and support her.

I desperately wanted to protect her beauty from men
who were polite, but dark prowlers behind fine suits.

She brushed back her long blond hair, fancied
my tennis bracelet on her thin wrist.

I saw then my protection of her was over.
Yet what protection did I have an evening long ago
when accepting this bracelet beneath a white chain arbor?

Melancholy Holiday

After walking through the snow sifted woods,
you haul loneliness, heavy as the fir dragged,
then pulled into your small living room.
You cannot decorate, but sit, smell the scent
of the tree, feel again strong wind pushing
your back to go forward, always forward ….
even if it is the holiday, two feet of snow tomorrow,
and you do not think you can feel anything, anymore,
for anyone.

Death of a Cowgirl

Every Sunday I went with my parents
to Sonny and Pat's vomit-scented house
where they drank themselves into oblivion.

A child of five, I brought a small pink suitcase of toys,
sat in a corner off the kitchen, watching
their faces turn into hideous masks.
They swore, staggered and smashed beer cans.
No one offered me a sandwich.
To escape the noise I went out to a dirt patch
shared by another house.

From there, a large pock-faced woman
asked if I wanted to be a cowgirl and play with her little boy
who twirled his felt cowboy hat while grasping
a belt with two shiny pistols.

I said yes, although my mother never
allowed me to play with other kids.

The woman held up a girl's outfit. I was so
excited, I gave her a hug. The son shared
a pistol and we pretended to shoot and ride horses.
Jumping up and down, I twirled my suede trimmed chocolate skirt.
The woman brought us lemonade.

Then I collided with my mother, screaming take off the foolish
clothes and get inside. I could not move. She threw the outfit
in the dirt, then pushed me down grabbing the white cowgirl boots,
telling everyone I could have been kidnapped or murdered!
This idea sobered them and we went home.

The Caretakers

There are caretakers that pray only to the moon at night,
Only when the moon is cold and in-love.
Tides wash down and blanket their children
Who do not sleepily roll in their beds,
Who do not dream.
And most of the caretakers are not old
Nor wise
Nor grieved.
They take care of life, and in doing that
They are busy and so full of peace—
They like peace and up righted people in spoons
And a little bit of death now and again to calm things.
They pray about that.

Yet, the caretakers do not like weeping.
They must care for the soul and the love
That tempers its weeping.
How may they touch and not feel the rivers?
Tide at their knees, now;
Dare they kneel and pray only to the cold and in-love moon?
O father, we are cold.
Let us rise.

Holiday Incident

It was near Christmas. A bare fir, we needed
permission from our mother to decorate,
leaned against the living room wall.
Yet, after what happened that day Nancy,
my older sister, just stuck a sparkle cardboard star on top.
The holiday was transformed forever.

Suffering from a migraine I awoke to mother screaming:
"get up, start scrubbing or there will be no holiday for
brats who deserve nothing!"

Nancy was eleven, fought with our mother the day before:
told her she did not know where our mittens and scarves were.
Our bedrooms were the size of closets. A turquoise
gauzy curtain in my room was frozen to the window panes
and wall. Mother came into my room, a cigarette dangling
in her mouth, pulled my arm hard until
I was shaking on the floor, crying my head hurt.
I threw up on my nightgown.
Nancy implored my mother for an aspirin,
but she disappeared and returned with a wire hanger.
"Lean over and take your punishment or I'll
slap her good!" Nancy did as she was told to protect me.
Gasping for breath, I crawled out of the room to wash up.
I could not help Nancy, my mother striking her paralyzed me.

Now I see the vision in black and white, a torn, frozen
curtain has glittery filaments. I crept into Nancy's room,
felt her head, gave her a Christmas bell pin, in case we did not
survive the season.

Who I Wanted To Be

Memory arises from a puckered,
bent photo of that day.
My cousin with her rich, sophisticated
family enter our shack, the abomination
of my stifled life.

We do not have enough chairs.
Children are left to stand or
crouch near the screen door.
I peek through a flimsy curtain
hanging as a door to my tiny room,
large enough for only a bunk
and a box for my folded clothes.

My cousin is eighteen. She wears
a light blue linen dress with a peter pan
collar, ankle socks and saddle shoes.
She twists the ringlets at her shoulder.
Her lavender scent reaches me as if
from another world where I belong.

They stay for one hour of laughter and talk,
then leave. I meant to speak to her, but
no one called me out and I had no shoes.
They will not be back. I saw
who I wanted to be and in a trance,
carefully refolded my clothes.

Old Companion

The moon sits in its mink of stars,
frets with shadow and light.
On men's shoulders perches like a lantern
during sleepless walking nights.
Its dark patches may mean it holds a grudge
or are stains of an unscoured cup.
Groaning, it shrinks and expands.
Your Highness or slave, the moon cannot give
back all you gave away: looks, a child,
the squandering of real emotion.
All your days it has astounded or derided you.
Yet, as an old companion you always forgive,
believe in its power to be the calm, all-seeing eye,
dressed to dazzle, reveal truths of your lone
imagination, then take you down to eternal dreams.

Fake Leopard Coat

My daughter arrives,
the princess
on Antigua Island.
She cups sand and feeds it
to the shell skirts of the ocean
she cannot conquer.

I buy her perfume
from a thousand ancestries.
Mannequins' clothes fill my arms
and enough jewelry to weld a crown.

Haunted by childhood memories
of poverty and an outdoor privy,
I was made to wear a torn, fake leopard coat to school.
On the playground cupped hands giggled at the spots.

I vow my daughter will never know the scourge
of winter bullying.
How I had to pounce, never land.

Insomnia

I lie down, wait for the whippoorwill
to return at dusk when hibiscus
have long since closed.

Nothing is heard but the cough
of the dream train moving,
brushing tree tips.

Sleep comes after one thought:
those who love me, will deprive me.
The body twists sheets in a Herculean form.

Nightmares weave vines
of fragments and frights. Sleep is snatched
in moments, as the mind struggles to awaken.

A disturbing presence disappears
at dawn. I arise haggard, haunted,
remember my name.

Farewell

I am so much a part of your life
I cannot see my own.
I felt the warm imprint of your fingers
on my tulip sleeves.
You never forget those sensations,
I cannot give in as I once did.
Resolute, I would rather keep the pale blossoms of memory.
A mentor was your role, minimal touch lit my mind.
Older now, strong winds push me to the edge. I will not succumb.
I no longer care for the advice you hide behind.
Go away. We are mismatched, despite all signs to the contrary.
A token stone necklace on a leather string reminds me
I am whole and distinct.

Best Friend

On Saturdays, I had an hour off from scrubbing.
I walked down our dirt road past shady maples.
A warm wind brushed my hair, the sky a tincture of grey.

Free, I twirled my outstretched arms then stopped,
did anyone see me?
More cautiously, I swung my arms, lifted my chin, wondered
if my girlfriend Molly, who moved far away, could see me?
I missed her breathless secrets, sitting next to me on the bus.

I told her I lived in a house where I could not laugh or talk.
She looked puzzled—

My mind could hide everything, even magical places.
I saw us together, holding hands at a white patio table,
facing a lake's hazy verdure trees upside down.
We sat in everlasting silence.

Then a perilous cloud grew in my chest.
I was late and ran back, my ponytail loosened,
wanting to gather my face in mother's skirts.
She turned away, scorned my loss.

The Parting

I try to remember the benches in the park,
One with a white glove left dangling,
The arthritic sycamore trees nearby and the
Afternoon I sat waiting for her to say goodbye.
There is never a parting without drama, but drama
Can also be silent. A pat on the hand, curling
A tendril around her ear, sharing a peach or
Just staring straight ahead, prolonging the end
With a trance. Separating forever mimics a
Pending death. Drama again.
She wanted it in the spring when bird calls
Disappeared into the cotton ball clouds and
Flowers' early perfume swirled until you
Were dizzy. I do not know which of us will
Be strong enough to go back to our former
Mates. Guilt never touched us. Now we
Must pay with our memories and lies,
Those scenes in the park of her dark red hair
Seen in the downpours of stellar rain.

Heart at Needlepoint

I have an impossible faith in you.
Leaving my seat by a window, I guardedly
search for you in uncomfortable places.

In a forest green tavern, bottles lined
with ornate seals, men boasting nonsense,
you might arrive at any moment. After years
of needlework, bent shoulders toward brilliant colors,
now I am a dark figure in the back.

Another day at an old arched bridge, I wait
until twilight holding binoculars to see you
strolling toward me in your cracked-leather jacket.
Blond hair cropped to your head, whistling as if
you did not wish to frighten me.

After pulling out stitches for a new beginning,
is it too late for initials on pillowcases?

The dream, at break-neck speed, cannot be stopped,
until a needle is pierced, down and back up, through the heart.

Hummingbird Date

I reminisce about us,
certain memories have become sacred
since our earliest days when I prayed for insight.

In Arizona, on our first outing, we walked through
an outdoor museum. Low hanging garden baskets
surrounded by hummingbirds beat out seconds.
Back and forth sipping nectar, they distracted
sudden feelings of love, until I grew dizzy.

The day briefly ignited concerns, I wondered:
was this forever or would it end with iced tea and sandwiches?

You suddenly disappeared, I panicked.
Where was the exit? Who would pay the hotel bill?
Then I saw you in the tourist line, buying a mute blue necklace.
Later placing it over my head, it was our first souvenir: but then
doubts spun—you were a decade older, divorced, had kids . . . .

It took a long time to slow my breathlessness.
I am still breathless.

Horse

I am walking toward the barn where I keep my horse.
My heart has been fluttering throughout the day.
The dogwoods and magnolias are in full bloom,
give nourishment to my essence barren all winter.
The horse is warm and content. Never having ridden him,
I pretend, no I know, we have a special bond.
We both tremble at my touch.

Never would I go near a barn where there is a horse.
Heart fluttering, I am afraid.
My fingers tremble when I grasp the diary that holds
my dreams and nightmares. I swear to you
some came true and connected me to my inner nature.

Does my passion grow flowers and create the horse?
Is faith the only guiding star I can cherish
when thinking of death?

The horse is running through a billowy cloud.
Suddenly it falls to the ground and dies.

Now the barn grows distant.

Red Fox

Along a row of junipers the startled fox
stared then quickly disappeared,
expecting me to find him.
It would take years since this was my first encounter.
From a car window I experienced most
of my early life.

I have a fairy tale life now—I love
and am loved. The first seventeen years,
except for school, I was nobody in a hostile,
drinking, violent, prowling familial pack.

When napping, I hide under a quilt and
feel safe as if living brings only harm.
Coming out of the fetal position, I see the soft
spring greens, images shudder in the breeze.

Branches drop fluffy clouds hung from strings.
The old folks are dead, I want to lie on the grass
and feel free as a red cardinal.
If I think hard enough for a long motionless time,
it might come true.

The Mermaid

I live in two worlds, half the stench of fish
half my hair bleaching on a rock.
It is lonely to fear land, not able to fully embrace
with my arms the wax and wane of adult love.
Some humans are afraid of the land, they sit like
statues in a trance wanting water to devour their
tragedies or just to deaden them.
It usually involves the loss of a child who never
learned to swim, yet who was taught to love water,
bobbing sailboats and nearness to the azure blue and
musical roar. Children see and believe in me and
I take them in, but they evolve into little fishes
and I am alone again.

The Rides

I must speak honestly of my father. He never
let us go hungry. Sweating tears of sawdust,
enough to fill his pant cuffs and in bitter
winter hacked ice bandages off limbs or went
to the town pantry for canned goods.

He had nothing to say to his daughters,
and only a few words to a punitive wife
who nagged he was mean, drunk and ignorant.
He could have left us.

We lived for his monthly drive
to Lilly's Grocery Store. Sometimes
we had to stay in the car, other times allowed to help.
We yearned for light and color, but could not buy
sewing materials, dolls, ribbons and barrettes.

Another splendid ride was to the dump.
A section of it was always burning, smoking embers.
The other part held recently thrown trash where
I found a clean tablet, allowing me to write,
saving my life.

Blackflies

The crows cawed out of their dark immensity.
Blackflies swarmed in clots of black.
I covered my head with a towel to see the ground.
My younger sister caught pneumonia that summer.
The doctor's bag smelled like mold. She was whimpering
as he listened to her chest, told my parents she could die,
then left twenty pink pills.
I fanned blackflies away from her face with a magazine.
To ensure her recovery, Mother fed her sweets and Pepsi.

School clothes, for me only, came from aunt's tired hand-me-
downs. I was the serious girl, saw my duty to fix my sister's life.
Dieting made her more ravenous to fill death's taunt.
School mates' cruel words like the flies, were too many
for her meager courage.

Morbidly obese, I watched her alone by her locker.
Leaving for college days later, she remained in her bedroom,
often wrote me letters without feeling, mere descriptions
of birds and pansies dying in the sun.

Calling her, I wept with alarm, still she ate doom:
morning, night and noon.

Magical Things

My grown brother is suffering
faraway in Maine.
I slowly look at pictures of us, choose
the happiest to place under my pillow.
An angel lit with good will hovers over me
with diaphanous wings, her cheeks pink
from the duties of a realm where wind
forms a cloud blue body, hair turns flaxen.

Understanding the eternal time photos
travel, I sleep as if it were balm for his
mental moods. When I awake I realize
the pictures on the floor have spilled
into their own destiny.

In one I am standing at a large boulder,
rolled down to our woods from
an ancient time. Later, his photo keepsake,
I am wearing bell bottom jeans, my hand
draped over the rock, sadness around my mouth.

Yet, I am happy: we are together,
not yet knowing I will have to leave him
with our abusive parents, still innocent of
heartbreak at four years old, believing in
angels flocking the night fields
amidst fireflies and other magical things.

Trucker Dream

I love it when the trucker hums by on
The distant highway at six every morning.
Feeling ecstatic our lonesomeness
Collides and no longer bedridden, I am in
That truck checking out his lunch bucket:
Two beef and pickle sandwiches, tasty cakes,
An apple, cokes and water. We sit so high,
I feel I am an astronaut looking down upon the earth.
It is exciting to bump across a Hudson River bridge.
The road spun black spirals, I shut my eyes, see
Iceberg Rose petals stained pink by dew drops.

The truck hit a pothole and I was afraid of awakening.
He was a dedicated driver. Divorced, for trucking was not his
Wife's style, he had one child. Seeing Charlotte kept him
Focused, even if he saw her once a month. He showed me
A picture. She had blond pig tails and a tiara
But there was a loneliness about her. I gave it back
Like it was the Queen's crown.
We went through nebulous fog, I was becoming
Sleepy, but I did not want to slip back into bed.
The Hudson River valley was reminiscent of its
Brilliant school of landscape painting.
The trucker was harder to hear. I think he asked
For a snack but I must have eaten all his food,
And before he found out, I woke up with
My quilt on the floor, haired snarled and
In need of my medication.
I was on Paul's "The Long and Winding Road."

First Journey

The day before entering high school I laid out
a blue flower blouse with a white Peter Pan collar.

I did not have high expectations, yet wanted to be
ready for a miracle. Happy I had grey eyes, nothing
else about my appearance was distinct.
Tragedy swirled in our kitchen like dust. The wood stove
spouted black smoke when my irate mother opened
the door. Abused, I was afraid of the stove hook, the broom,
sticks of wood, and wire hangers.

My pencil box was in a macramé handbag. It was ugly
bright orange with red stars. Dad brought it home from
the slow burning grounds of the dump which looked
ominous and sad at night. I was reading about the Civil War,
how their small campfires scattered the night illuminating
horror and carnage.

It was 1965 and so little was noble and right. I, so alive and young,
welcomed the September acorns mounding on the ground.

Aware of my small, innocent life I hoped,
walking the dirt road to the bus stop, high school would be
wonderous and exciting. I believed prayer had made me lucky,
assured someone was listening.

In the back of the room during English class, my shawl tangled on
a chair. I saw an erasure tossed hard over my head, hitting Azel
Nichols who could not read. His failure, the torn wing of an angel
as real as a blue jay slicing the sky or shiny black crows dancing
on high wires.

After class, dazed but determined, I spoke to the teacher about
his throwing the erasure, how harmful and unholy it was.

The Bed and the Boat

Old now, the bed is my world,
I am wrapped and tangled as if
In a cocoon.

I remember when it was time to settle in
Bed, a place to rest the body, not an invisible
Cage where hours inch the black arrows of
A grandfather clock inlaid with gold leaves.

If the silence of my room was the same as
A quiet forest after rainfall, I might heal.

I have haunting thoughts of loved ones when
Our bodies danced in circles through the
Mighty duties of each day.

High pillows bring hands together
In suspended prayer.
I recall granddaughter, Sienna Justine,
Her little fingers touching my face.
Where is she now?

If I could hold her,
We would be drifting in a red boat laughing
As we near willows, and boats with beautiful
Names—Apple Shed, Buttercup Bee.
Lullabies and her cooing gliding over the water.

Baby Doll

My uncle wants to play tag in an Aroostook
County potato field. I ran away from him
until he fell drunk against a barrel.
I cling to my father but he kicks me away
like his beer can.

Life was never mine, I just wandered in
with my doll to keep an eye on me,
one I could also protect.
No one looks out for me.
Even the baby doll that sees everything,
does not bat an eyelash.

Nanny

Clouds moved slowly as a train in snow.
Needed no more, four immaculate days left,
I run to hold the infant of my employer.
The father had flown in the wind as a
white paper cut out.

A nanny was my destiny for two decades.
Why now do I feel deprived of this child
I wish to smother with furtive kisses
fusing us together?

It will only get worse
for I cannot find this adoration again.
Was I a child over or under loved?
Barren, no longer a handsome woman,
where can I seek solace for this loss?

Wet lashes, rise and fall in gentle breathes.
Oh, I loved hard, grieved harder than
anyone would ever know. Trembling I packed
my bags. A nanny's duty served, they thought,
with appropriate affection and no more.

Winston Arthur Berry

When my infant brother died at birth, I retreated to the rear of the red shed near the tall, human-like sunflowers and smoked a cigarette.

Relatives were drinking quietly as if he would awaken. The little cinnamon cakes and black berry crepes were untouched.

I had to crawl into my own grief, no one to take my hand. The old ladies with large handbags dug into them for hankies.

When I breathed in the smoke, I felt strangely calm. Somewhere I was lost in shock beneath the bent sunflower faces.

I had plans for him—rocking, picnics, spinning the old gyro top, pulling my rusty wagon.

Then I realized he would still have a life, for angels have a way of weaving things together as now a brisk wind made the sunflowers flap their leaves.

Seeds fell in a spray of bright confetti to the soft ground.
I had another cigarette and the visions for us flew with crows overhead.

I now sat, my back against the hot shingles, the loss did not seem real anymore or was this a trick of grief?

Old Bath Road, Maine

I was fifteen, wrote
A poem about an Indian woman
Who spit, swore, but was kind
To an impoverished girl who
Thought her a lady.
My English teacher sent the poem
To *The New Yorker* where it
Was published.

Stressed daily, I had to shampoo
My hair with greasy Ivory soap, brush
My teeth with baking soda, and
Nightly wash my one pair of panties.
I slept in a chair that made my neck
Feel wrapped in a round oatmeal box.
Poverty built my character and empathy.
I thought everyone lived like this.

I went down to the Sheepscot River flats
To watch the backs of worm diggers appear as
Stumps with curved, short hoes in hand.
Digging deep and fast, they moved across
The mud flat in high boots.
Every Friday they spent all their earnings.

Our trash gleamed with beer cans and liquor bottles.
Drinking, my family said shocking things or
Divulged secrets. It was maudlin theatre.
Escaping under the bed we had front row seats.
We learned about dead dreams, bad deeds.
I smelled like a stale cigarette.

Then I won a poetry contest and met a famous poet.

I Remember Birches

I do not know what my English teacher
saw in a plain, impoverished student who
at fifteen published a poem in a magazine she
had never heard of—*The New Yorker,*
and lived in a shack, half-paralyzed by
violent drunks shouting words they meant,
could not take back.

In grey halls, he stopped to give me
lists of books to read, colleges I should consider,
a critic of my last poem.

With a chaperone he drove me to Middlebury College
in Vermont. I remember the stark white birches, crossed
with thin black lines in a scaffolding of parchment,
limbs leaping to cathedral heights in the sky.

The writing house of Robert Frost was not far away.
I rarely rode in a car, felt the rapture of climbing
a mountain past boulders dented with dark shadows.
Was I losing my way toward a culture I was not
yet part of?

Inside a heavy brick building, we met the head
of the English Department, smiling and nodding
over my poems. Brutally shy, I could not speak,
attired in itchy wool, brown hair in a long braid.
My chaperone, a pastor's daughter, yawned in the corner.

On the drive down the mountain, the birches cascaded
in a mauve twilight beauty. Home, family asleep, I slid into
bed under several thick coats. The house was smaller:
one poem had moved heaven and earth.

About the Author

Born into a logger's family in Wiscasset, *"The Prettiest Village in Maine",* she illuminates the dark side of its youth. Many poems deal with the challenges she and others faced: lack of education and love, abuse, alcoholism, and poverty. A supportive high school English teacher and a poem in *The New Yorker* at age fifteen, led to degrees from *Mount Holyoke College, Hollins College, and Drexel University.* Often returning to her family and the natural beauty of Maine, she maintains compassion in her work for those who could not leave the burdens of their families for a better life.

Her first book *Cruel Roses,* was published in 2018. Also an abstract watercolorist, she lives and writes in Doylestown, PA.

www.ingramcontent.com/pod-product-compliance
Lightning Source LLC
Chambersburg PA
CBHW071359090426
42738CB00012B/3166